MATH. READING. SUCCESS.

ABOUT KUMON

What is Kumon?

Kumon is the world's largest supplemental education provider and a leader in producing outstanding results. After-school programs in math and reading at Kumon Centers around the globe have been helping children succeed for 50 years.

Kumon Workbooks represent just a fraction of our complete curriculum of preschool-to-college-level material assigned at Kumon Centers under the supervision of trained Kumon Instructors.

The Kumon Method enables each child to progress successfully by practicing material until concepts are mastered and advancing in small, manageable increments. Instructors carefully assign materials and pace advancement according to the strengths and needs of each individual student.

Students usually attend a Kumon Center twice a week and practice at home the other five days. Assignments take about twenty minutes.

Kumon helps students of all ages and abilities master the basics, improve concentration and study habits, and build confidence.

How did Kumon begin?

IT ALL BEGAN IN JAPAN 50 YEARS AGO when a parent and teacher named Toru Kumon found a way to help his son Takeshi do better in school. At the prompting of his wife, he created a series of short assignments that his son could complete successfully in less than 20 minutes a day and that would ultimately make high school math easy. Because each was just a bit more challenging than the last, Takeshi was able to master the skills and gain the confidence to keep advancing.

This unique self-learning method was so successful that Toru's son was able to do calculus by the time he was in the sixth grade. Understanding the value of good reading comprehension, Mr. Kumon then developed a reading program employing the same method. His programs are the basis and inspiration of those offered at Kumon Centers today under the expert guidance of professional Kumon Instructors.

Mr. Toru Kumon
Founder of Kumon

What can Kumon do for my child?

Kumon is geared to children of all ages and skill levels. Whether you want to give your child a leg up in his or her schooling, build a strong foundation for future studies or address a possible learning problem, Kumon provides an effective program for developing key learning skills given the strengths and needs of each individual child.

What makes Kumon so different?

Kumon uses neither a classroom model nor a tutoring approach. It's designed to facilitate self-acquisition of the skills and study habits needed to improve academic performance. This empowers children to succeed on their own, giving them a sense of accomplishment that fosters further achievement. Whether for remedial work or enrichment, a child advances according to individual ability and initiative to reach his or her full potential. Kumon is not only effective, but also surprisingly affordable.

What is the role of the Kumon Instructor?

Kumon Instructors regard themselves more as mentors or coaches than teachers in the traditional sense. Their principal role is to provide the direction, support and encouragement that will guide the student to performing at 100% of his or her potential. Along with their rigorous training in the Kumon Method, all Kumon Instructors share a passion for education and an earnest desire to help children succeed.

KUMON FOSTERS:

- A mastery of the basics of reading and math
- Improved concentration and study habits
- Increased self-discipline and self-confidence
- A proficiency in material at every level
- Performance to each student's full potential
- A sense of accomplishment

▶▶ GETTING STARTED IS EASY. Just call us at 877.586.6671 or visit kumon.com to request our free brochure and find a Kumon Center near you. We'll direct you to an Instructor who will be happy to speak with you about how Kumon can address your child's particular needs and arrange a free placement test. There are more than 1,700 Kumon Centers in the U.S. and Canada, and students may enroll at any time throughout the year, even summer. Contact us today.

FIND OUT MORE ABOUT KUMON MATH & READING CENTERS.
Receive a free copy of our parent guide, *Every Child an Achiever,* by visiting kumon.com/go.survey or calling 877.586.6671

Sipping Juice

Drink the juice by pulling ❶ down.

1. Cut along ▬▬▬ .

2. Fold downwards along ▬ ▬ ▬ .
   Cut along ▬▬▬ and unfold.

3. Slide ❶ into the
   bottom of ❷.

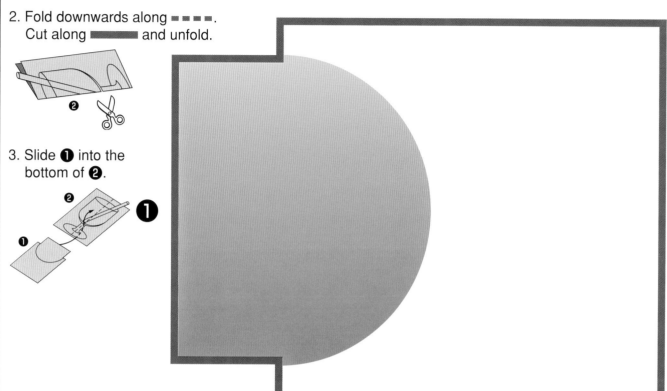

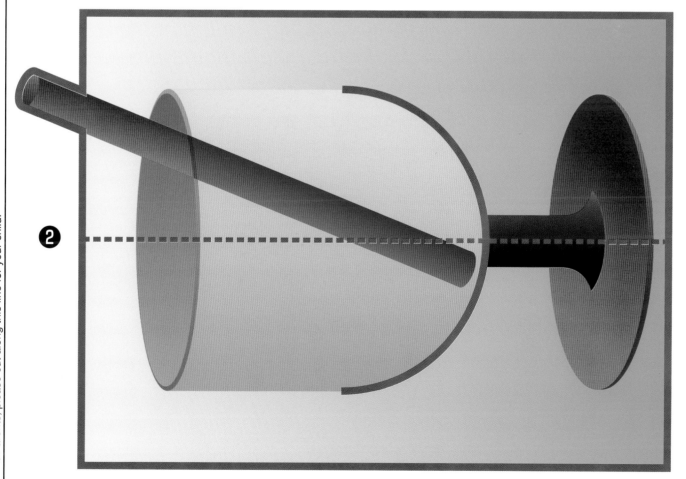

❷

Animal Wrestlers

HOW TO PLAY

Put the animals on a box, and tap the box to see them fight.

1. Cut along .

2. Fold upwards along ▬ · ▬ · ▬.

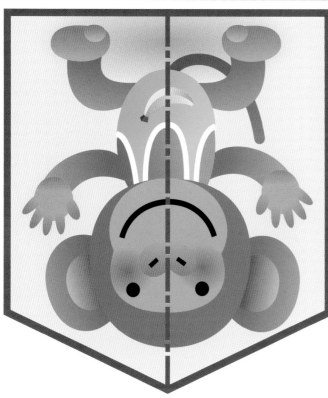

Rolling Racers

1. Cut along ━━━━.

2. Fold downwards along ▬ ▬ ▬.
   Curl a-❶ into a ring, and put glue
   on 📋A to paste the ends together.

3. Put glue on 📋B and paste a-❷ onto
   a-❶.

● Repeat the steps above with the pieces
  labeled with "b" to create a second craft.

Blow from behind. Let's race!

HOW TO PLAY

b-❷

a-❷

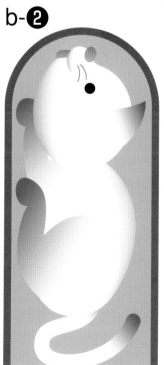

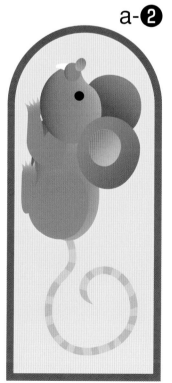

b-❶

a-❶

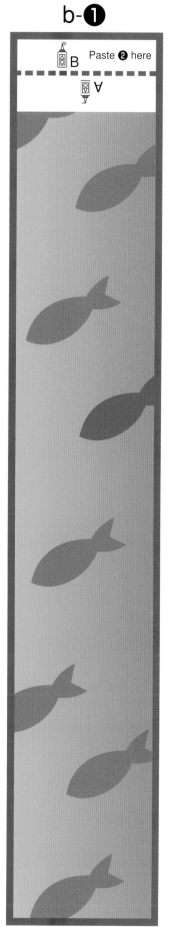

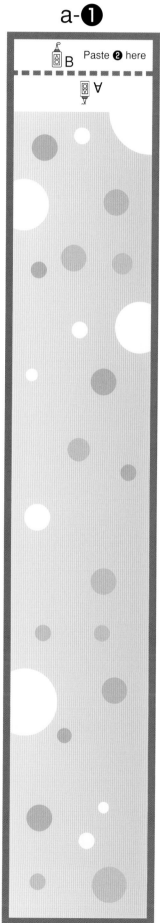

📋B   Paste ❷ here

📋A

📋B   Paste ❷ here

📋A

A Funny Clown

1. Cut along ▬▬▬.

2. Fold downwards as shown below and cut along ▬▬▬.

3. Fold downwards along ▪▪▪▪ and upwards along ▬▪▬▪.

Hold the paper as shown below to make the clown move.

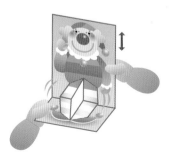

Time for a Change

❷

❸

1. Cut along ▬▬▬.

2. Fold downwards along ▪▪▪▪.

3. Turn ❶ over and put ❷ on the back of ❶.

HOW TO PLAY

Change the faces, hats, clothes, and legs. You can also use ❸ to make a very strange clown!

❶

Rolling Panda

HOW TO PLAY Hold the paper as shown, and let it roll forward. Watch the panda roll on the table!

1. Cut along ▬▬▬.

2. Fold downwards along ▪▪▪▪ and upwards along ▬▪▬▪ in the order as shown below.

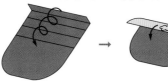 →  →

＊Parents, please cut along this line for your child.

Green Means Go!

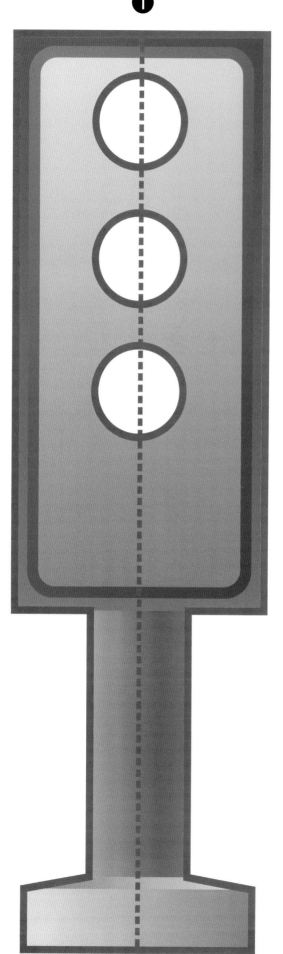

❶

1. Cut along ▬▬▬.

2. Fold ❶ downwards along ▬ ▬ ▬ .
   Cut out the circles and unfold.

3. Fold ❷ downwards along ▬ ▬ ▬ .
   Paste ❷ onto the back of ❶.

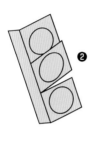

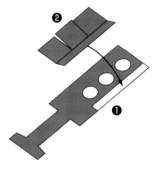

HOW TO PLAY

Change the traffic light from green to yellow to red and make all the cars stop.

❷

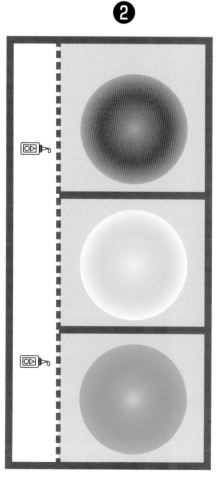

Waving Long Nose

8

1. Cut along ▬▬▬▬.
2. Fold downwards along ▬ ▬ ▬ ▬.
3. Attach ❷ and ❸ to ❶.

HOW TO PLAY

Pinch the back of the elephant with your fingers and rub the sides together. The elephant will wave his nose!

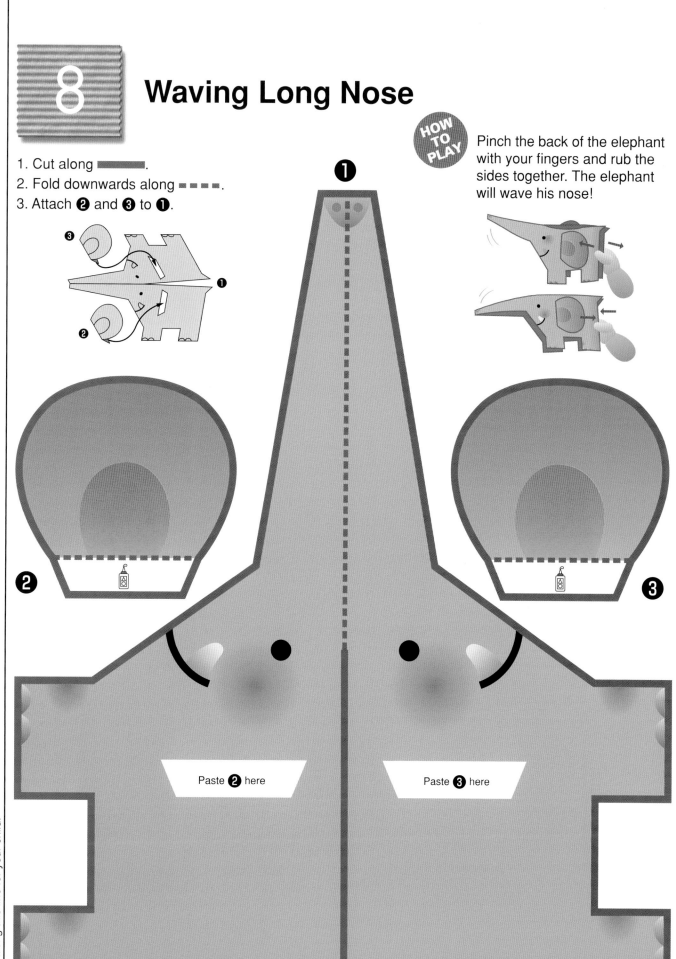

❶

❷   Paste ❷ here

❸   Paste ❸ here

9 A Bear Lumberjack

1. Cut along ▬▬▬.

2. Fold downwards along ▬ ▬ ▬
   and upwards along ▬ ▪ ▬. Attach
   ❶ and ❷ to ❸ as shown below.

HOW TO PLAY
Push and pull the flaps as shown below. The bear will chop the wood.

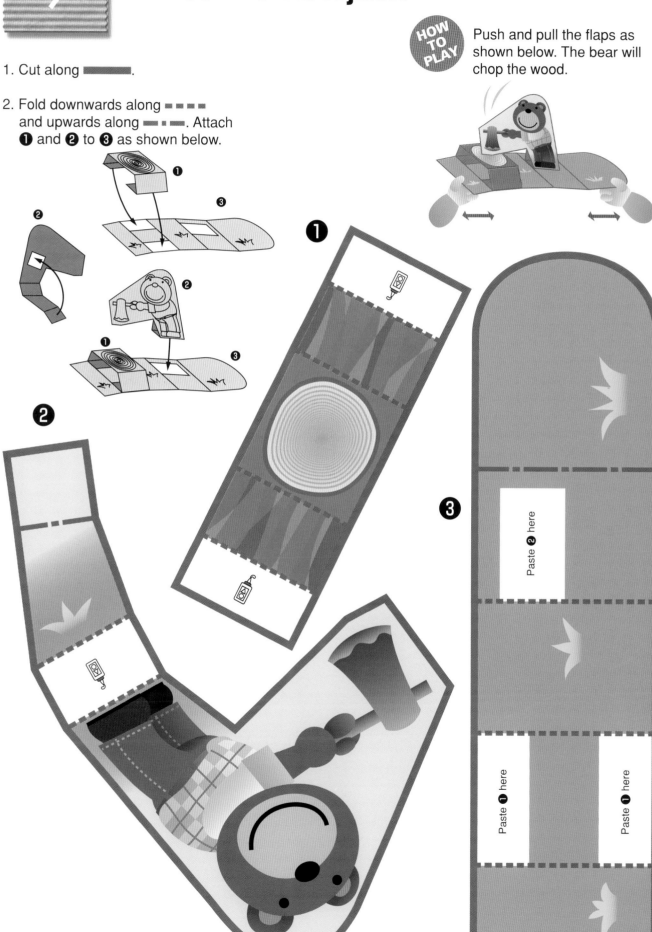

Paste ❷ here

Paste ❶ here

Paste ❶ here

*Parents, please cut along this line for your child.

Soccer Star

1. Cut along ▬▬▬ .
2. Fold ❶ and ❷ downwards along ▬ ▬ ▬ , and paste the tabs onto the back of each leg.
3. Curl the top part of ❸ (🖊C) around and paste its back onto 🖊A. Curl the bottom part of ❸ around and paste its middle to 🖊B. Continue curling the remaining section of ❸ around and paste it to 🖊C.

HOW TO PLAY

Put your first and middle fingers into the holes and kick the ball like a soccer star!

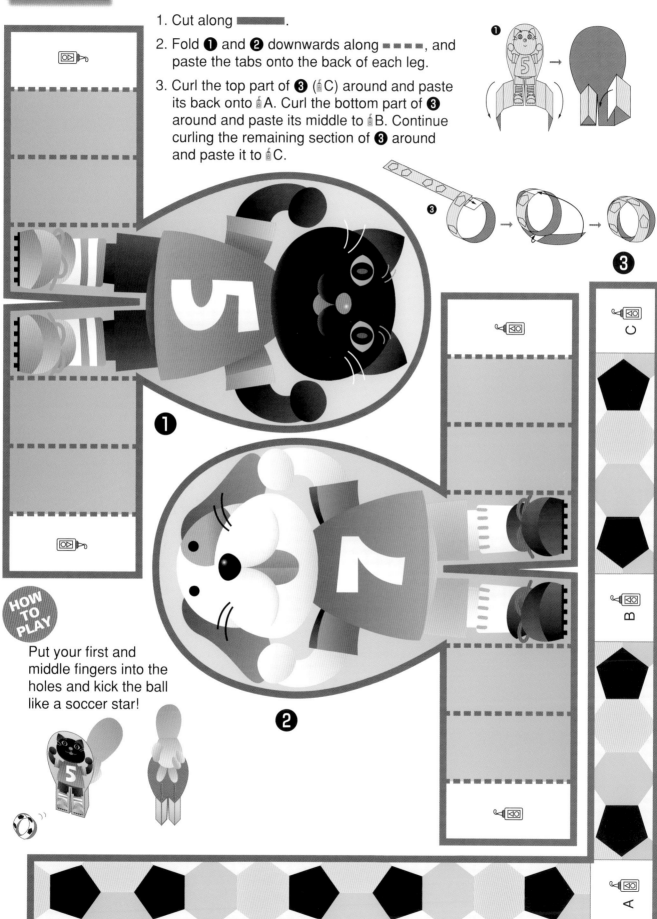

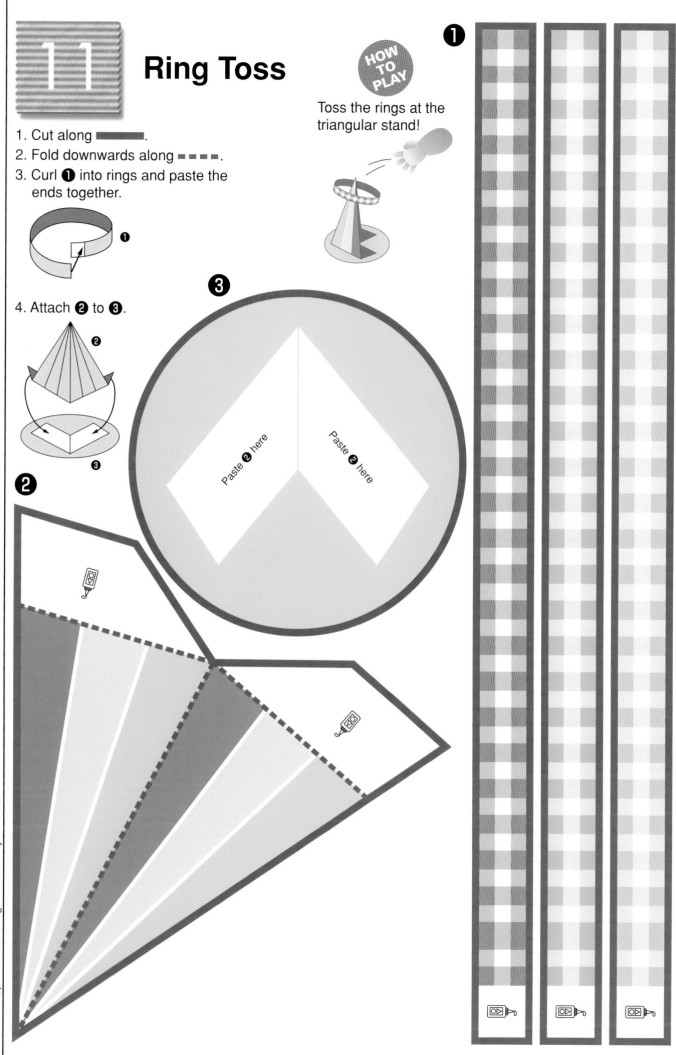

11 Ring Toss

1. Cut along ▬▬▬.
2. Fold downwards along ▬ ▬ ▬.
3. Curl ❶ into rings and paste the ends together.

4. Attach ❷ to ❸.

HOW TO PLAY

Toss the rings at the triangular stand!

❸

Paste ❷ here   Paste ❷ here

❷

❶

*Parents, please cut along this line for your child.

Clap Your Hands!

1. Cut along ▬▬▬.

2. Fold ❶ downwards along ▪ ▪ ▪ ▪ and paste it to ❷.

3. Fold ❸ and ❹ downwards and upwards according to the lines, and then paste the two parts together as shown.

4. Attach ❸ and ❹ onto ❶ and ❷.

Hold the hands with the white tab as shown, and push and pull the sleeves repeatedly.

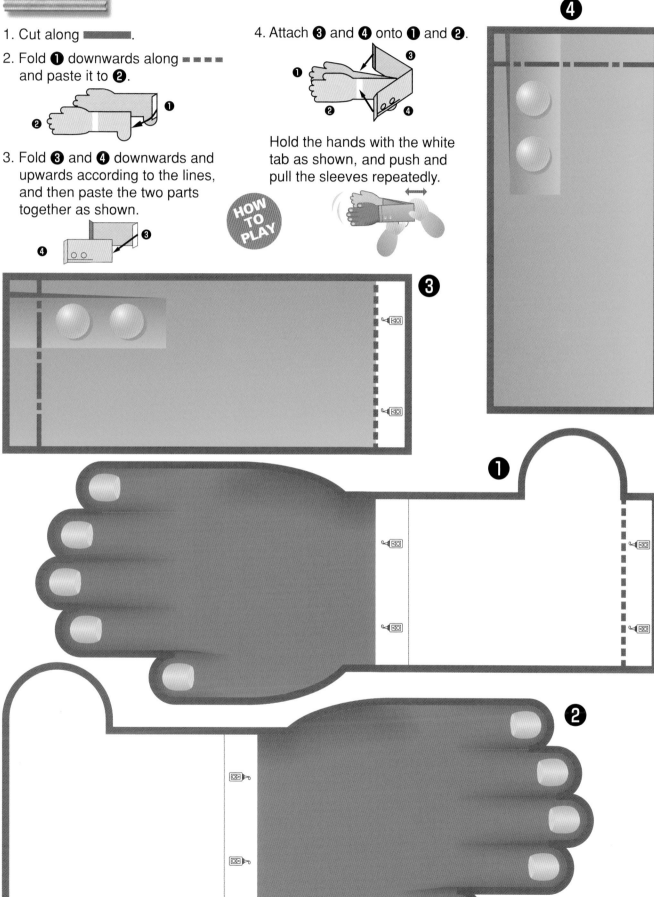

Croaking Frog

1. Cut along ▬▬▬.

2. Fold downwards along ▬ ▬ ▬ ▬
   and upwards along ▬ · ▬ · ▬.

3. Paste ❶ and ❷ together.

HOW TO PLAY

Push and pull the side flaps to make the croaking frog open and close his mouth.

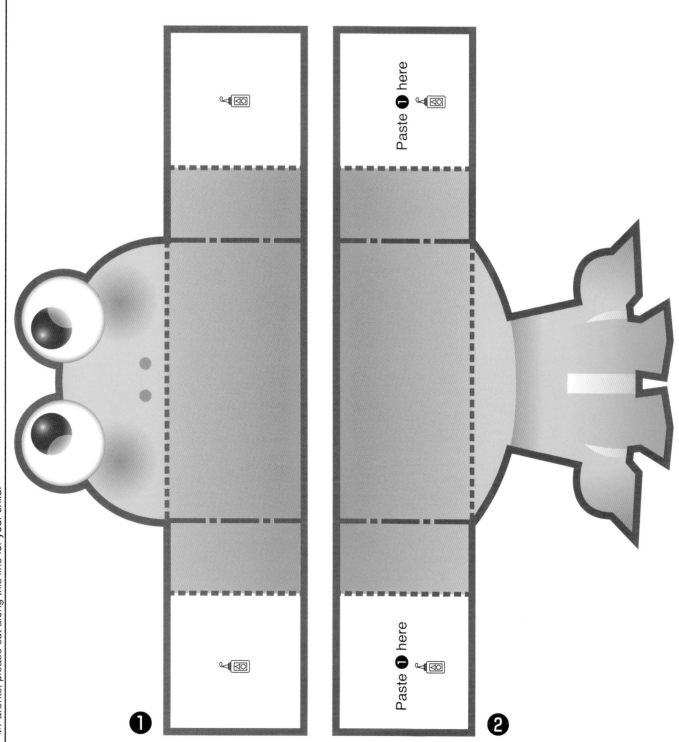

Paste ❶ here

Paste ❷ here

❶

❷

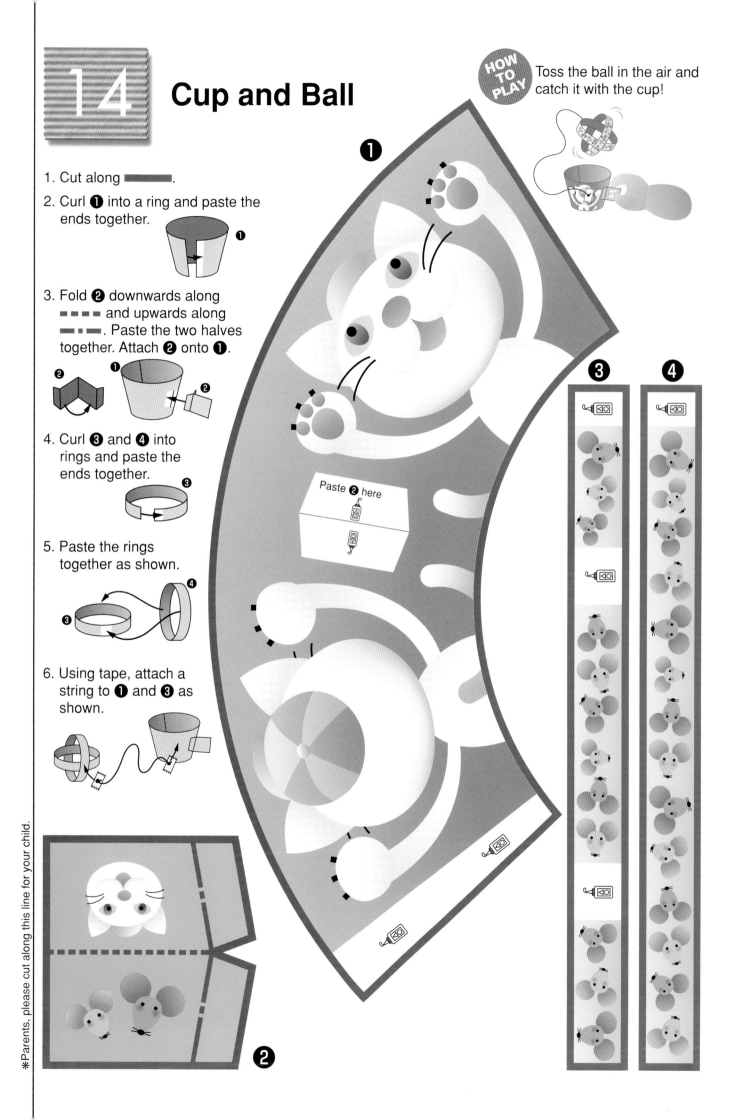

14 Cup and Ball

HOW TO PLAY — Toss the ball in the air and catch it with the cup!

1. Cut along ▬▬▬▬.

2. Curl ❶ into a ring and paste the ends together.

3. Fold ❷ downwards along ▬ ▬ ▬ ▬ and upwards along ▬ ▪ ▬ ▪ ▬. Paste the two halves together. Attach ❷ onto ❶.

4. Curl ❸ and ❹ into rings and paste the ends together.

5. Paste the rings together as shown.

6. Using tape, attach a string to ❶ and ❸ as shown.

Paste ❷ here

❶

❷

❸

❹

Rocket Launch

1. Cut along ▬▬▬.

2. Fold downwards along ▬ ▬ ▬ ▬.

3. Curl ❶ and paste the ends together. Attach ❷, ❸, and ❹ to ❶.

4. Make two slight cuts along the short lines on ❷. Insert a rubber band into these grooves as shown in the picture.

HOW TO PLAY

Push the rocket down on a cardboard toilet paper roll and let go. The rocket will blast off!

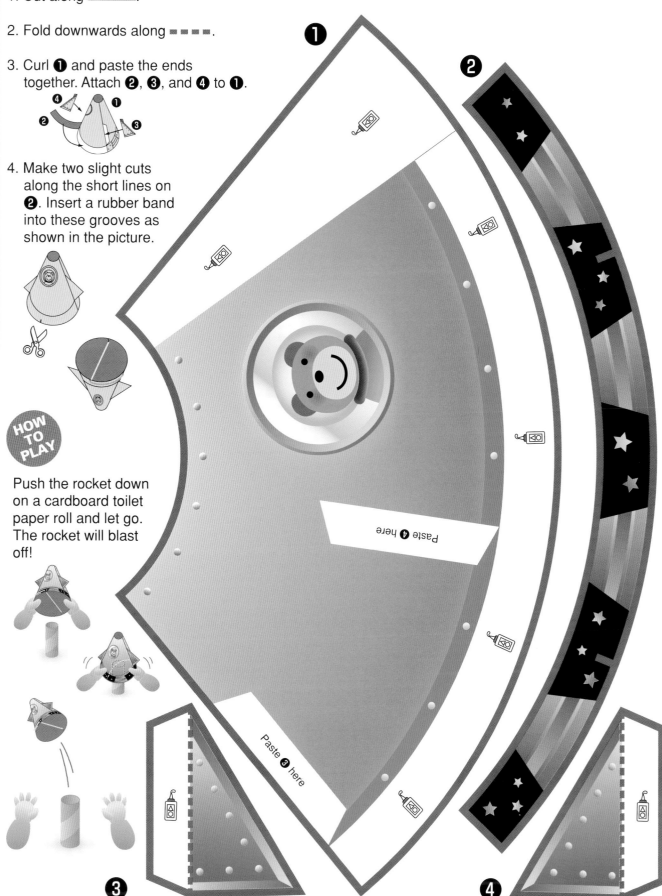

Paste ❹ here

Paste ❸ here

❶

❷

❸

❹

16 An Angry Gorilla

1. Cut along ▬▬▬.

2. Fold downwards along ▬ ▬ ▬ and upwards along ▬ ▪ ▬ ▪.

3. Attach ❷ and ❸ to ❶ by lining up the edges. Then attach ❹ to ❶ as shown below.

HOW TO PLAY

Hold down the green part of ❶. Push down on it, and the gorilla will look angry.

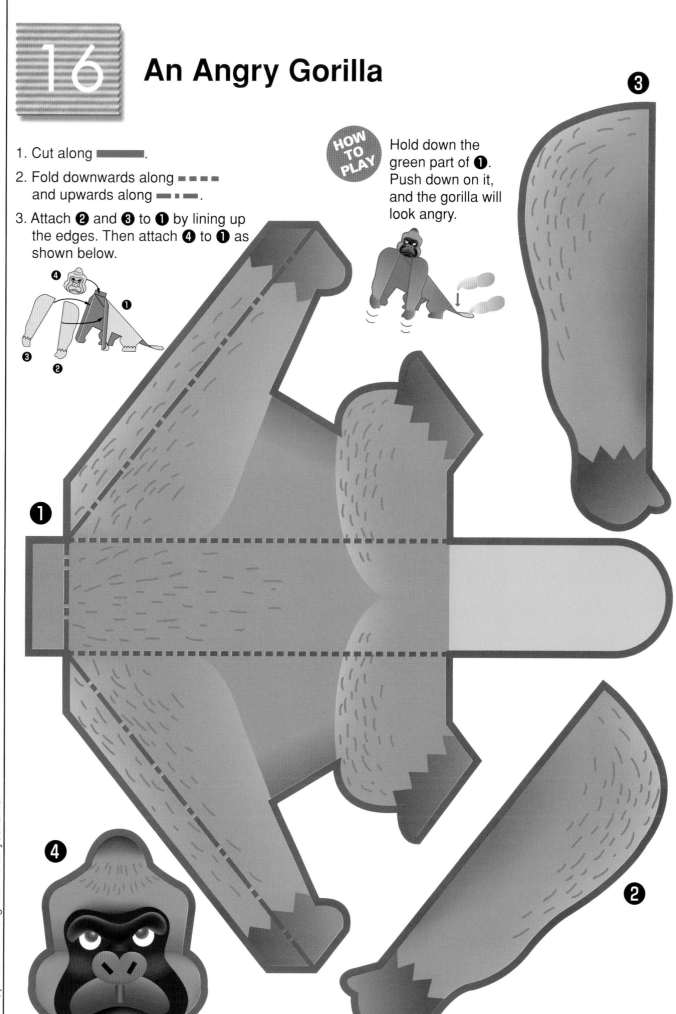

Birthday Card

HOW TO PLAY Open the card to get a birthday surprise!

1. Cut along ▬▬▬.

2. Fold downwards along ▪ ▪ ▪ ▪ and upwards along ▪▬ ▪ ▬ ▪.

❷

3. Make a slight cut along the short lines on ❶ and ❷. Then insert these grooves into each other.

4. Attach ❶, ❷, and ❸ to ❹ as shown below.

❶

❸

❹

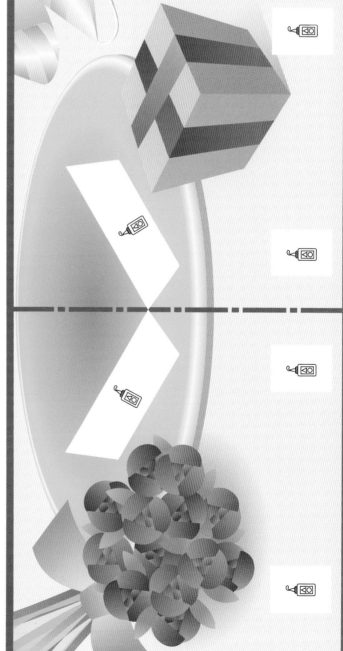

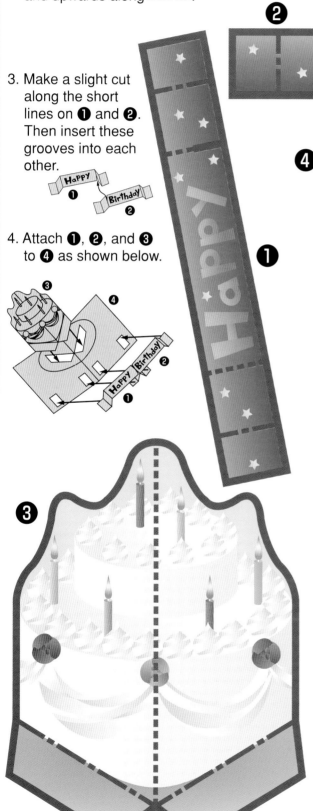

*Parents, please cut along this line for your child.

A Sea Otter with a Clam

1. Cut along ▬▬▬.

2. Fold downwards along ▬ ▬ ▬ and upwards along ▬ ▪ ▬ ▪ ▬.

3. Attach ❷ and ❸ to ❶.

4. Put glue on the back of ❷ and ❸, and attach ❹ to them.

HOW TO PLAY

Push and pull the side flaps. The sea otter will try to break the clam on the rock.

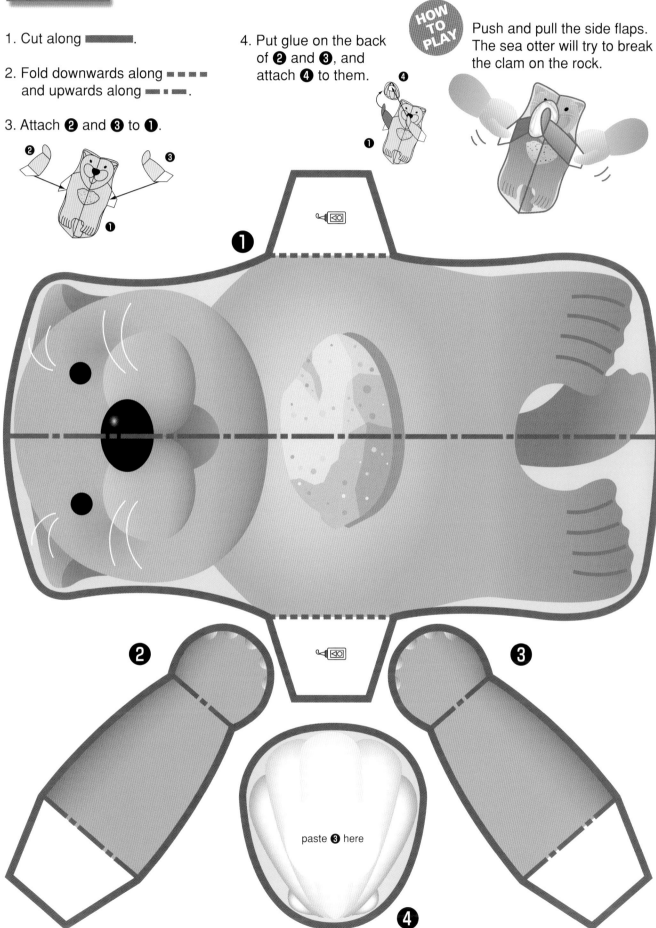

paste ❸ here

Spinning Top

1. Cut along ▬▬▬.

2. Fold downwards along ▬ ▬ ▬ ▬
   and upwards along ▬·▬·▬.

3. Attach ❷ to the back of ❶ as
   shown below.

HOW TO PLAY

Blow from obliquely above
and watch the top spin.

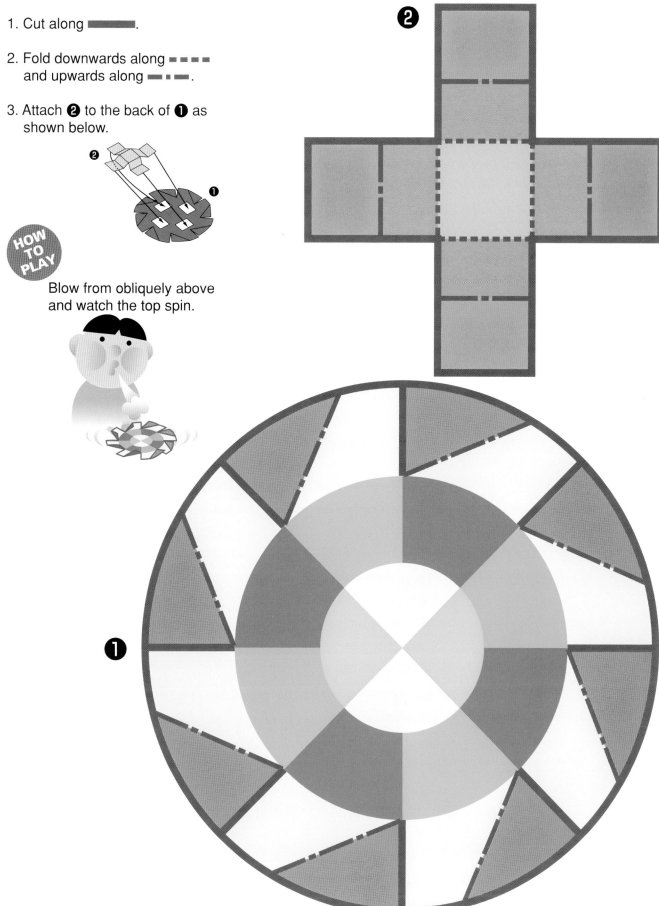

Leap from the Elephant's Nose

HOW TO PLAY

Hang the animals on the elephant's nose. Pull his nose back - when you let go, the animals will jump. Try to land them in the ring!

1. Cut along ▬▬▬.
2. Curl ❶ and ❷ and paste the ends together.
3. Fold ❸ downwards along ▪▪▪▪ and upwards along ▬▪▬▪. Attach it onto ❹.
4. Fold ❺ downwards along ▪▪▪▪ and upwards along ▬▪▬▪.

❺

❹

❶

❷

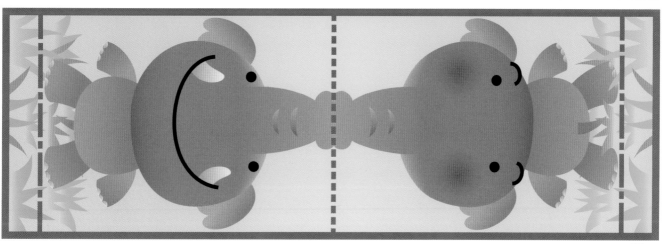

*Parents, please cut along this line for your child.

❸

Man or Wolf?

1. Cut along ▬▬▬.

2. Fold downwards along ▪▪▪▪
   and upwards along ▬▪▬▪.

3. Attach ❷ and ❸ to the back of ❶
   as shown below.

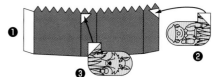

4. Paste the edges of ❶ together.

HOW TO PLAY Shift the box from side to side and
you will see the man turn into a wolf.

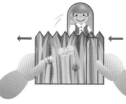 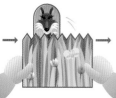

❶

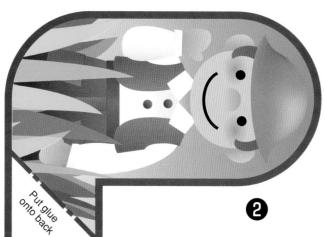

Put glue onto back

❷

Put glue onto back

❸

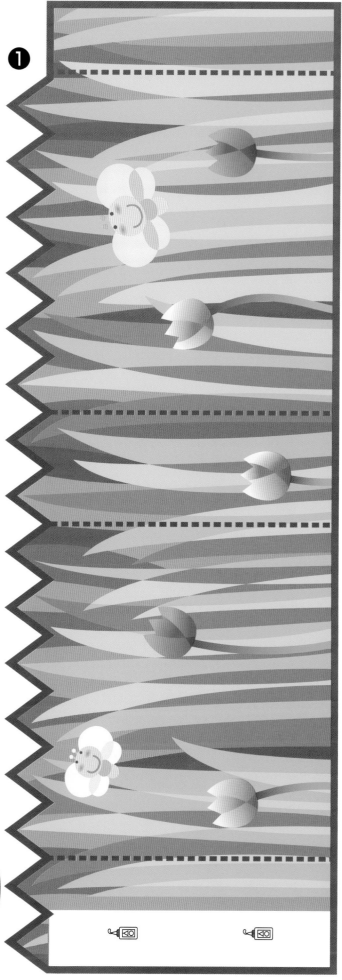

Monkeys with Fans

1. Cut along ▬▬▬.

2. Fold upwards along ▬ ▬ ▪ ▬ ▬.

3. Attach a-❶ to a-❷ as shown.

● Repeat the steps above with the pieces labeled with "b" to create a second craft.

Hold the monkey as shown and move your thumb from side to side repeatedly. The monkey will fan you!

HOW TO PLAY

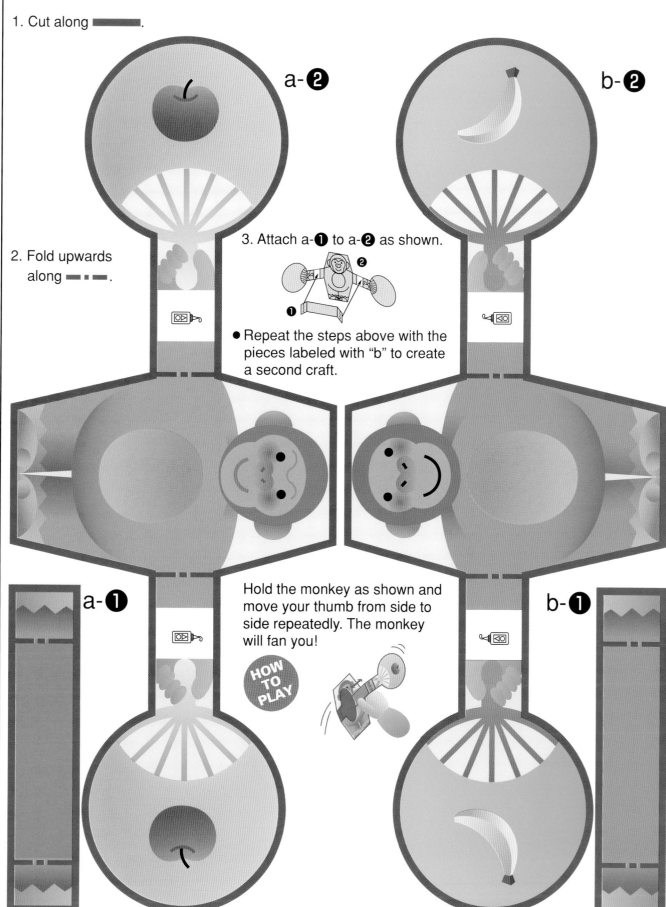

A Tulip Blooms

1. Cut along ▬▬▬.
2. Fold downwards along ▬ ▬ ▬ and upwards along ▬ ∙ ▬.
3. Put glue on the back of ❶ and paste it to the back of ❷. Then attach ❶ and ❷ to ❸ by pasting 🖊A to A and 🖊B to B.

4. Paste the tab to complete the flower pot.

HOW TO PLAY

Hold the tab below the flower pot. Push it upward, and watch the tulip grow.

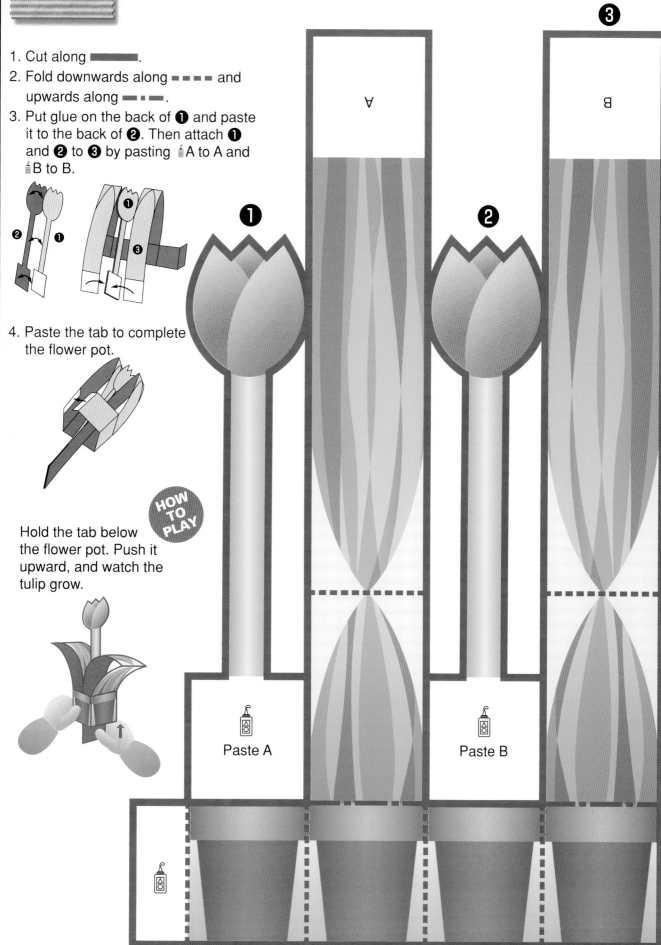

A

B

❶

❷

❸

Paste A

Paste B

Fun on the Slide

1. Cut along ▬▬▬▬.
2. Fold downwards along ▬ ▬ ▬ and upwards along ▬ · ▬ · ▬. Paste the tabs to complete ❶.
3. Attach ❷ and ❸ to ❶ as shown.

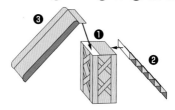

4. Paste the tab to complete ❹.

❶

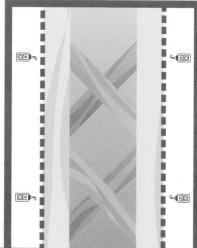

❹

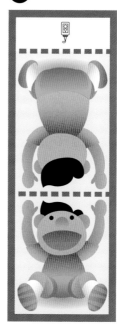

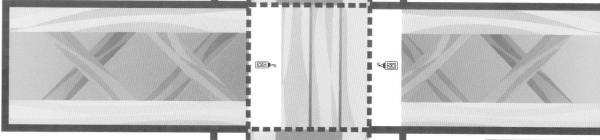

HOW TO PLAY Watch the boy slide!

❷

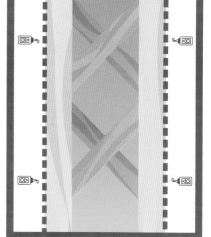

❸

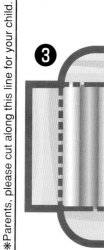

25 Shark Attack

1. Cut along ▬▬▬ .

2. Fold downwards along ▬ ▬ ▬ and upwards along ▬ ▪ ▬ ▪ .

3. Put glue on 🧴A and 🧴B and attach ❶ and ❷ to the back of ❸ as shown.

4. Paste ❶ and ❷ together using 🧴C. Paste the tab to complete ❸.

5. Paste the backs of ❹ together. Then attach the fin to ❸.

Push and pull the shark's tail. Watch out for the shark's bite!

HOW TO PLAY

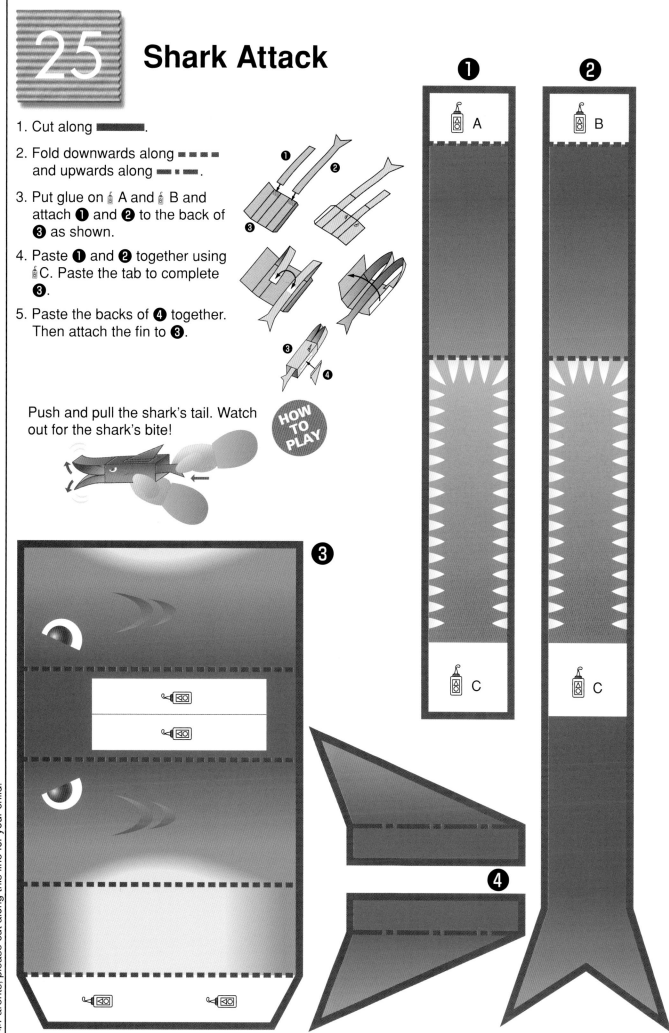

A Conveyor Robot

1. Cut along ▬▬▬.

2. Fold ❶ downwards along ▬ ▬ ▬ ▬ and upwards along ▬ ∙▬ ∙▬. Cut a hole in the back of ❶ as shown below.

3. Fold ❷ downwards along ▬ ▬ ▬ ▬ and insert it into the hole in the back of ❶.

4. Paste ❷ to the arms of ❶.

5. Fold ❸ downwards along ▬ ▬ ▬ ▬ and paste the tab to complete the part.

6. Attach ❶ to ❸.

7. Fold ❹ downwards along ▬ ▬ ▬ ▬ and paste the tab to complete the part.

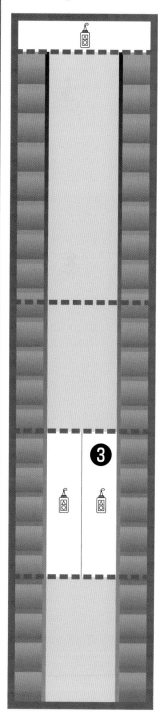

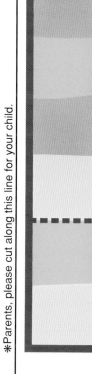

❹

❶

❷

❸

HOW TO PLAY

Push ❷ while holding ❸ to make the arms move. Pick up the goods!

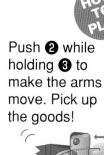

Leap, Frog!

1. Cut along ▬▬▬.

2. Fold ❶ downwards along ▬ ▬ ▬ and upwards along ▬ ▪ ▬ ▪.

3. Paste the tab to complete ❶. Then attach ❷ as shown.

4. Fold ❸ downwards along ▬ ▬ ▬ and upwards along ▬ ▪ ▬ ▪. Paste the tabs to complete the part as shown.

Put ❸ on ❷ as shown. Then push down on ❶. When you let go, the frog will leap to the lily pad!

HOW TO PLAY

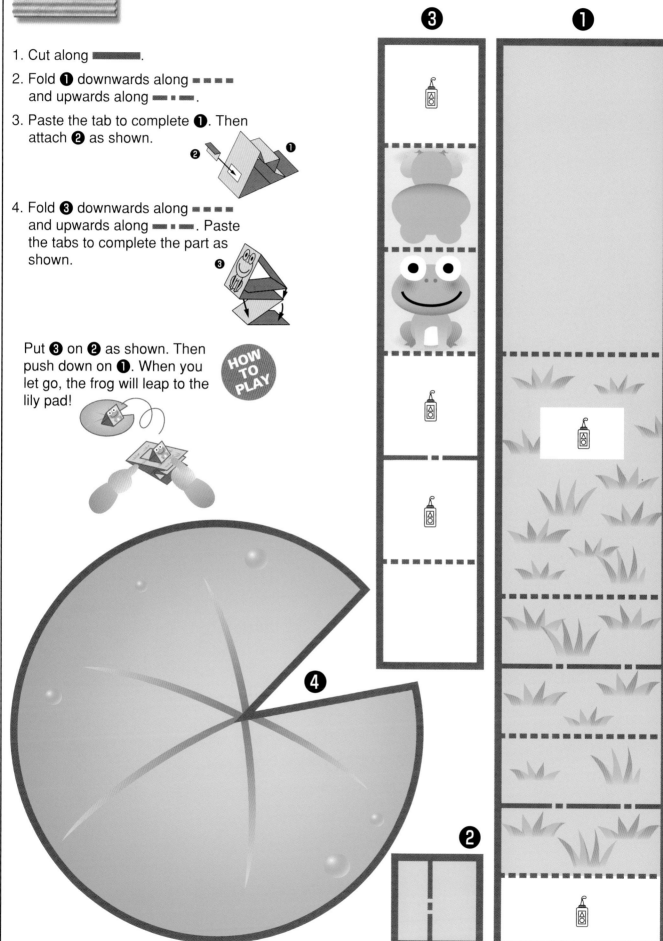

Bulldozer

1. Cut along ▬▬▬▬.

2. Fold ❶ downwards along ▬ ▬ ▬ ▬ and upwards along ▬·▬·▬. Paste the tabs to complete the part as shown below.

3. Fold ❷ and ❸ downwards along ▬ ▬ ▬ ▬. Curl the pieces, then paste the tabs as shown.

4. Attach ❷ and ❸ to ❶.

5. Fold ❹ downwards along ▬ ▬ ▬ ▬. Paste the tabs to complete the part.

6. Fold ❺ downwards along ▬ ▬ ▬ ▬ and upwards along ▬·▬·▬. Paste the two halves together in the middle. Attach the tabs at the end of ❺ to ❹.

7. Insert ❺ into ❶.

Use ❺ to move the shovel as you operate the bulldozer.

HOW TO PLAY

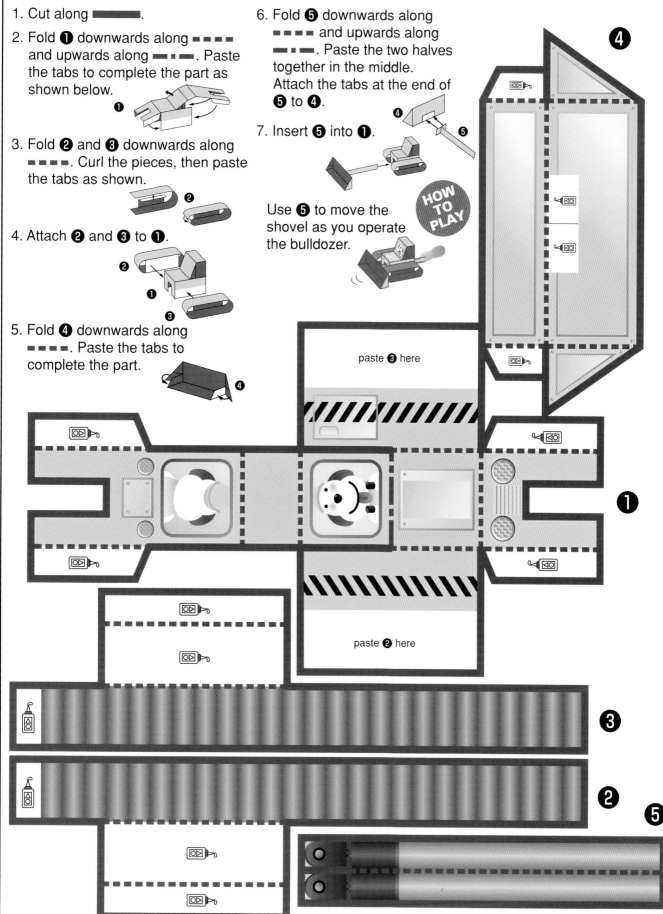

paste ❸ here

paste ❷ here

❶ ❷ ❸ ❹ ❺

Blast Off

1. Cut along ▬▬▬.

2. Fold downwards along ▪▪▪▪
   and upwards along ▪▪—▪▪—.

3. Attach ❶ to ❷ by pasting 🖊A.
   Then attach ❸ to ❶, and ❹ to
   ❷ by pasting 🖊B.

4. Put glue on 🖊C and
   paste ❸ and ❹
   together. Then attach
   ❺ to ❸ and ❹.

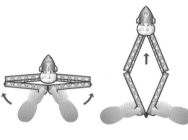

HOW TO PLAY

Hold ❶ and ❷ at the bottom and move the pieces as shown below. Watch the rocket blast off!

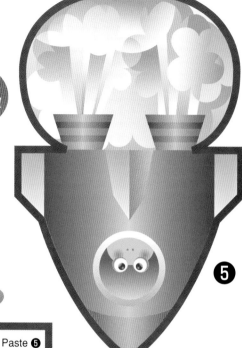

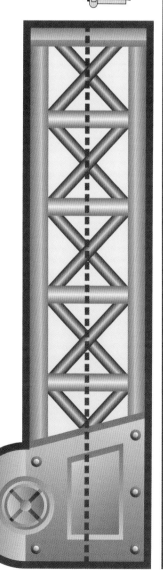

❷

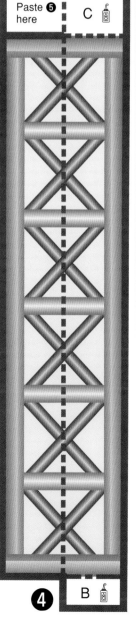

Paste ❺ here   C 🖊

B 🖊

❹

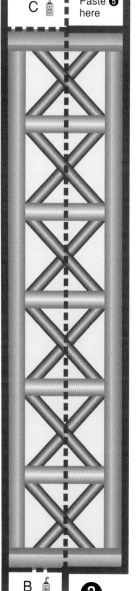

C 🖊   Paste ❺ here

B 🖊

❸

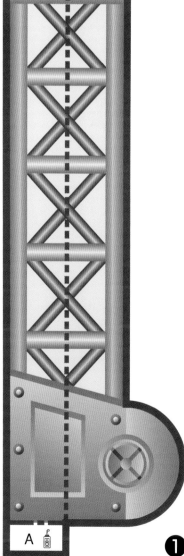

A 🖊

❶

❺

*Parents, please cut along this line for your child.

Seesaw

1. Cut along ▬▬▬▬.

2. Fold downwards along ▬ ▬ ▬ ▬
   and upwards along ▬ ▪ ▬ ▪ ▬.

3. Attach both pieces of ❷ to the
   back of ❶ as shown below.

Line up the
parts at the
center of ❶.

❶
❷

4. Attach ❸ to ❹.

❸
❹

5. Paste ❷ and ❸
   together.

❷
❶
❸
❸

6. Attach ❺ to ❶.

❺ ❶ ❺

HOW TO PLAY

Push down on one
side of ❶ and watch
the animals seesaw.

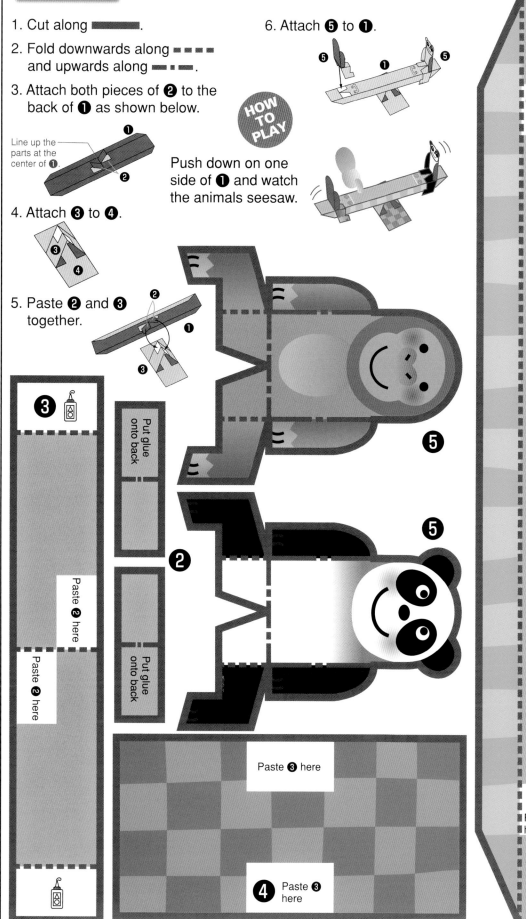

❸

Put glue onto back

Paste ❷ here

Paste ❷ here

❷

Put glue onto back

❺

❺

Paste ❸ here

❹ Paste ❸ here

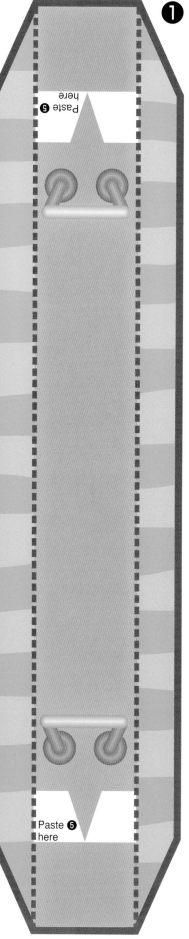

❶

Paste ❺ here

Paste ❺ here

Twisting Parachute

1. Cut along ▬▬▬.

2. Fold downwards along ┅┅┅ and upwards along ▬·▬·▬.

3. Attach a-❷ to a-❶.

HOW TO PLAY

Drop the parachute and watch it twist as it falls.

4. Attach a-❶ to a-❸ as shown below.

- Repeat the steps above with the pieces labeled with "b" to create a second craft.

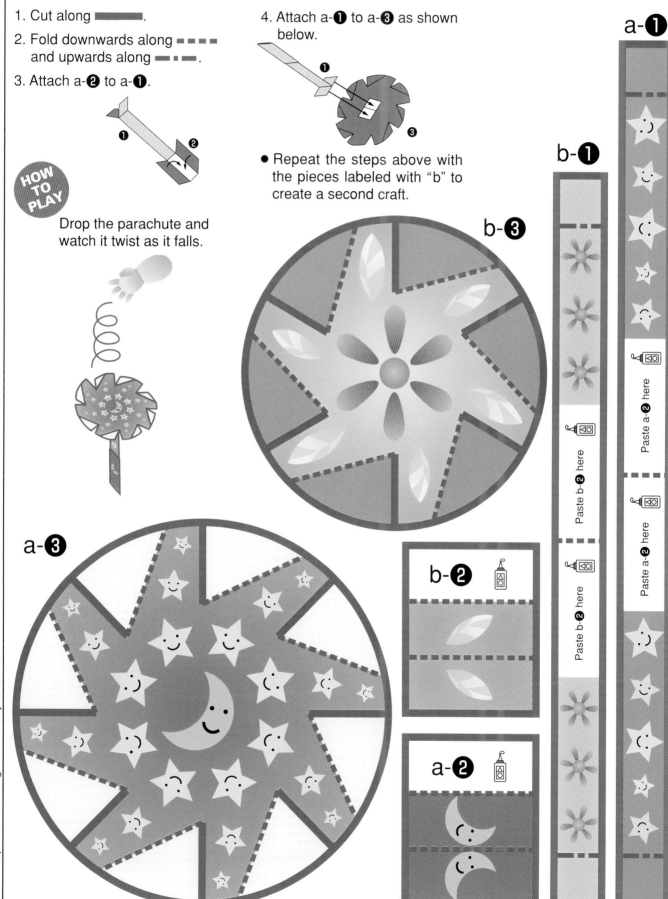

a-❶

b-❶

b-❸

b-❷

a-❷

a-❸

Paste b-❷ here

Paste a-❷ here

Paste b-❷ here

Paste a-❷ here

Paste b-❷ here

A Hungry Anglerfish

1. Cut along ▬▬▬.

2. Fold ❶ downwards in the middle and cut out the hole along ▬▬▬.

3. Fold downwards along ▬▬▬▬ and upwards along ▬▬•▬.

4. Thread ❷ through the hole in ❶ and attach it to ❸.

5. Attach ❹ to the front of ❸.

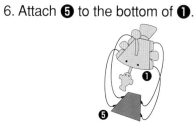

6. Attach ❺ to the bottom of ❶.

HOW TO PLAY

Pull its tail and the anglerfish will eat the smaller fish.

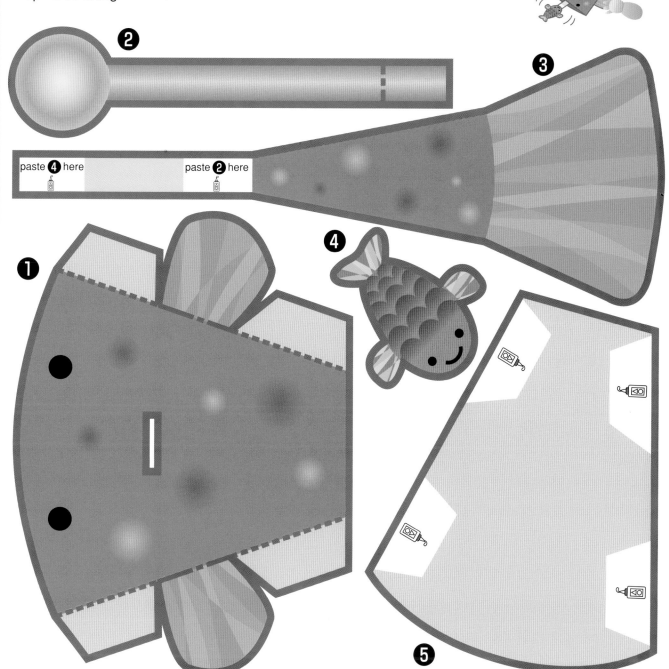

❷

❸

paste ❹ here

paste ❷ here

❶

❹

❺

Certificate of Achievement

is hereby congratulated on completing

My Book of Amazing Crafts

Presented on _____ , 20___

_____
Parent or Guardian